"IS THIS REALLY HAPPENING?"

Twenty five years without hitting the skins? Can you really have a few weeks' rehearsal and then get behind a kit at a major venue and play before thousands and please the critics? - Bearing in mind that you only have to breathe in slightly wrong before the British press are ridiculing every breath you take.

I've never seen Luke play the drums. I saw him do his first acting role in "Plan 9 from outer space" in a theatre in Southend, I saw him in a musical play called "What a Feeling" where I saw him sing for the first time, and he can sing well. I saw him play Danny Zuko in "Grease", and I went to surprise him in Prague when he was filming his first acting role in a Hollywood film, playing the main villain opposite Wesley Snipes in "Blade 2", but I've never seen him hit the skins.

I still had to wait til the summer to see him do it in rehearsals.

I took these pictures whilst he was getting ready for the press conference, we didn't talk that much as I didn't want to make him nervous or distract him from what was about to happen.

New Haven Publishing Ltd

Email: newhavenpublishing@gmail.com

director:
teddie@newhavenpublishingltd.com

rights:
jan@newhavenpublishingltd.com

Website:
newhavenpublishingltd.com

Published 2021
All Rights Reserved

::

::

Cover and interior design © Pete Cunliffe
pcunliffe@blueyonder.co.uk

Copyright © 2021 McVirn Etienne

ISBN 978-1-949515-07-7

newhaven publishing

25 YEARS...

25 years of knowing a couple of friends but yet never having seen them perform together.

Having spent the last two and a half decades having some great fun and witnessing the births of different careers away from what they were involved in before I met them, I was intrigued to see if I would be able to find out if I could get anywhere near to seeing the pandemonium & fan adulation they had in the eighties, but never witnessed first hand.

I wasn't disappointed, I was impressed, and I was happy and pleased for my friends. I'm not a writer so will find it a little difficult to convey into words exactly what it was like.

But I am a photographer, and a picture tells a thousand words. I hope the pictures you're about to see in this book can somehow convey the feeling of the hard work that's involved in putting a concert together to please your diehard fans.... and to confront your fiercest critics.

This is a photographic record of the day the comeback was announced, the road to getting things together, the rehearsals, to learning to play with each other again, and the joy on people's faces whilst they relive their youth.

Enjoy.

INTRODUCTION

"HELLO? HAVE YOU HEARD?"

" Hello?" "Have you heard? The band are getting back together! Luke agreed to it, he wants to do it!"

This is how the phone call I got from a mutual friend in the early hours one morning went, and I was totally taken by surprise to be honest. Its well documented that Matt had for a long time wanted to do a reunion and complete unfinished business but Luke was reluctant to do so. He had left the music business behind and embarked on a very successful acting career in Hollywood with gusto and passion, whilst Matt had a successful run in Caesar's Palace, Las Vegas, and still loved and enjoyed singing. So let me get this right, the two of you haven't performed together in over twenty five years, Matt has spent almost a decade singing live music in Vegas but singing in a totally different style than in his pop days, whilst Luke

has not picked up his drumsticks for over twenty five years, but now you're going to announce that you're playing two gigs in the Indigo O2 Arena in London? I've never seen them play together, as I became friends with them just after they split up, but could they pull it off?

The UK press undeservedly had given them a harsh time at every turn, and this could have been just another opportunity to rip them to pieces. I spent the last twenty-five years taking pictures of both of them for various projects, but never photographed them together.

There was no way on earth I wasnt going to be there to document it.

And before you know it, TV presenter Emma Willis, who was a die hard Bros fan, is announcing the gigs would be happening the following year. The first gig sold out in under ten seconds.

"I'VE GOT ONE WEEK..."

"One week to get to a good standard of drumming before I even rehearse with the band, then Matt arrives a week or two after! Thats not long."

And to top it all he's got a documentary crew filming him non - stop plus my ugly dreadlocked mug popping flashguns in his face while he's practising. Now that would get on my nerves I can tell you, but it needs to be done, it needs to be documented. What I thought would happen, and what would be normal for anyone, was for Luke to struggle initially.

Anyone would be struggling after not playing for so long, right?

But what surprised me was how naturally good Luke was, He seemed to float just right into it. But there was still a long way to go, being a drummer is the hardest working role in a band, one mistake and you can throw the whole band off, so you have to be as tight as you can be.

I CAN SEE, THIS IS NO JOKE

Just because Bros were a teenage pop band in the eighties, it does not mean that they were going to treat this gig as some teenybop comeback gig.

They had a point to prove, that they could play & that they can sing. I must admit Luke is putting the hours in rehearsals, today was one of the first days I saw him smile because I believe it was one of the first days that he felt it all coming together.

It's been hard work and the work is tiring.

REHEARSALS AT JOHN HENRY'S STUDIO...

The band have already practised for one day. It's the first time I've seen Matt face to face for about eight years. We lost touch with each other, distance sometimes does that to friendships, but it was really good to see him as we reminisced a bit about old times.

But they're not here to chit chat, as they have work to do. There seems to be a nervous energy in the air but that slowly disappears as they begin to warm up.

Matt has been in the country about a day, and despite knowing them for so many years, this is the first time I've ever seen them play together.

They begin to play and I'm expecting it to be a bit disjointed as they've only spent a day together. I am pleasantly surprised as they seem to get into their groove very quickly, with a much harder rock sound than I was expecting.

This is a bit weird for me as although I'm in a room half filled with people I know, there was a tense nervousness in the air.

It's almost as if the boys had a point to prove to their friends and their fans, and to each other as well.

After all its been nearly thirty years, if I could mind read it's almost as though Matt was thinking,

"I'll show you all I can still sing"

and Luke was thinking;

"I'll prove to you all I can play."

BURNING POINT...

In my opinion thats exactly what it was on a few levels. Artistic differences, changes in the songs, all of these things can happen at rehearsals & build frustration between people.

An over long drum fill section which is murder to complete, and totally takes it out of you when you're a drummer. It's the drummer who usually signals the end of the fill, or so I thought. But this one went on too long and I think at that point Luke wanted to end that fill a bar or two earlier as it was taking its toll and he made it obvious he wanted to change it. It showed in his face and emotions. Muscle burn when you're playing any instrument kills your body.

But at that point everything changed, the band took a break & chilled for lunch. When everyone came back they started the set again, and everything clicked. The band were tight, the vocals were on point, the backing singers made a big difference too and ad-libbed a section which really worked. It was as if the previous week's tension had lifted from the room, everything was quite jovial & cheerful after this day.

I guess you could call it a cathartic moment, but after the previous couple of days it was a welcome change.

When you're photographing something like this, you want to capture every emotion but at the same time when you're trying to produce something creative & semi-documentary you want to be real but at the same time please the people you're shooting with their permission which shows them in a real but good light. It's human nature to want that.

The documentary film makers were in a different position than me, they would be capturing "warts and all" situations that I had no access to or indeed desire to capture to be brutally honest. After all, these were my friends and I wanted them to succeed in what they were trying to achieve.

The day for the O2 rehearsal was getting nearer, and I was glad that I could get close to the rehearsals, especially near Luke as I knew during the gig I wasnt going to get any close shots of him & get plenty of Matt. I wanted to even the balance in what I was producing, even though a book was not planned at any stage whatsoever, I wanted a balance of pictures I was producing between them.

O2 ARENA REHEARSAL

It's a buzz watching a band practice their set, it's also a learning curve seeing what actually goes on to get even the simplest of songs to sound right & tight. Every little percussion strike, a slightly long note, an extra cymbal crash, an unnecessary guitar riff. Every single little thing is looked on in great detail.

But who is to say who is playing to loud? Or who has come in a fraction late? Should it be more pop, like the record, or a bit more rock?

It's at times like these when tension or frustration can rise, well if it didn't you're not human, & boy did it rise!

Although it looks like everyone has to obey the front man, (James Brown springs to mind) if the band have rehearsed a song, all its beats & chords & signal strikes, a band can be thrown if they've only been playing together for a couple of weeks instead of months on tour.

I had it in my mind that Matt was singing with a totally new band compared to the band he's been playing with for the past year or two, who maybe would suddenly start ad libbing a groove like some bands do. People can get tired and they can get snappy with each other. It's funny - if you're with friends in a restaurant and things get a little tense you can tell everyone to calm down, behave etc.

When you're in someone's place of work under their invite, if there's a heated discussion going on that you're uncomfortable with, you either leave or shut the f*** up.

But thats what happens in a creative proces I guess, I dunno. I work by myself 90% of the time so what I say goes, but with twins it's a whole different story.

I felt a shift in the air initially, that's all I'm saying.

Call it sibling rivalry, call it creative differences, whatever you like. But on a basic level the way I saw it was two siblings, who live in the same country but don't spend a lot of time together, and who have carved out success away from each other, but have not played together in decades, of course there is going to be a little tension in the room.

Matt is the front man, running around with the mic, singing his heart out. Luke is behind a massive drum kit, partially hidden from view on stage (which worries me a bit come the gig, because I need clear pictures of him there) but there is no doubt that Luke's role is immensely important as the WHOLE band rely on him not missing a beat! He will probably be the hardest working band member there, as it is very tiring mentally & physically playing non stop almost for two hours.

Of course everyone is working hard, very hard. But hitting those skins repeatedly on time with all your limbs takes it out of you. But you only get the sense of how hard it is when you're standing next to a musician in the rehearsal room. Even harder when you try it yourself like I did and failed miserably. I play a bit of guitar & that strains your fingers & arms, but drumming is something else.

When the drums & bass kicks in, especially when it's heavy, you can't help but nod your head and tap your feet. But I have to say when Matt kicks in with his voice & lays a sweet melody over the kicking drums & bass, it brings it all in tight. His voice is still remarkably good, and the pop melodies over the heavier rock sound is a good marriage.

I'm enjoying this O2 rehearsal.

HITTING THE SPOT

Thats exactly what the boys are doing... hitting the spot. And this is only the rehearsal.

So far so good and no mistakes at all, I know the stadium is empty this time round and a massive crowd is going to add adrenalin, but a crowd will aid the sound as it will stop the echo hitting back into the band which surely must be off putting. But I must say it's sounding great. But what's very important for me is I'm getting to know the highlights of the show to photograph.

I have a chance to at least guess where Matt is going to be to get good angles of him, and also at what point both he and Luke will be in the frame.

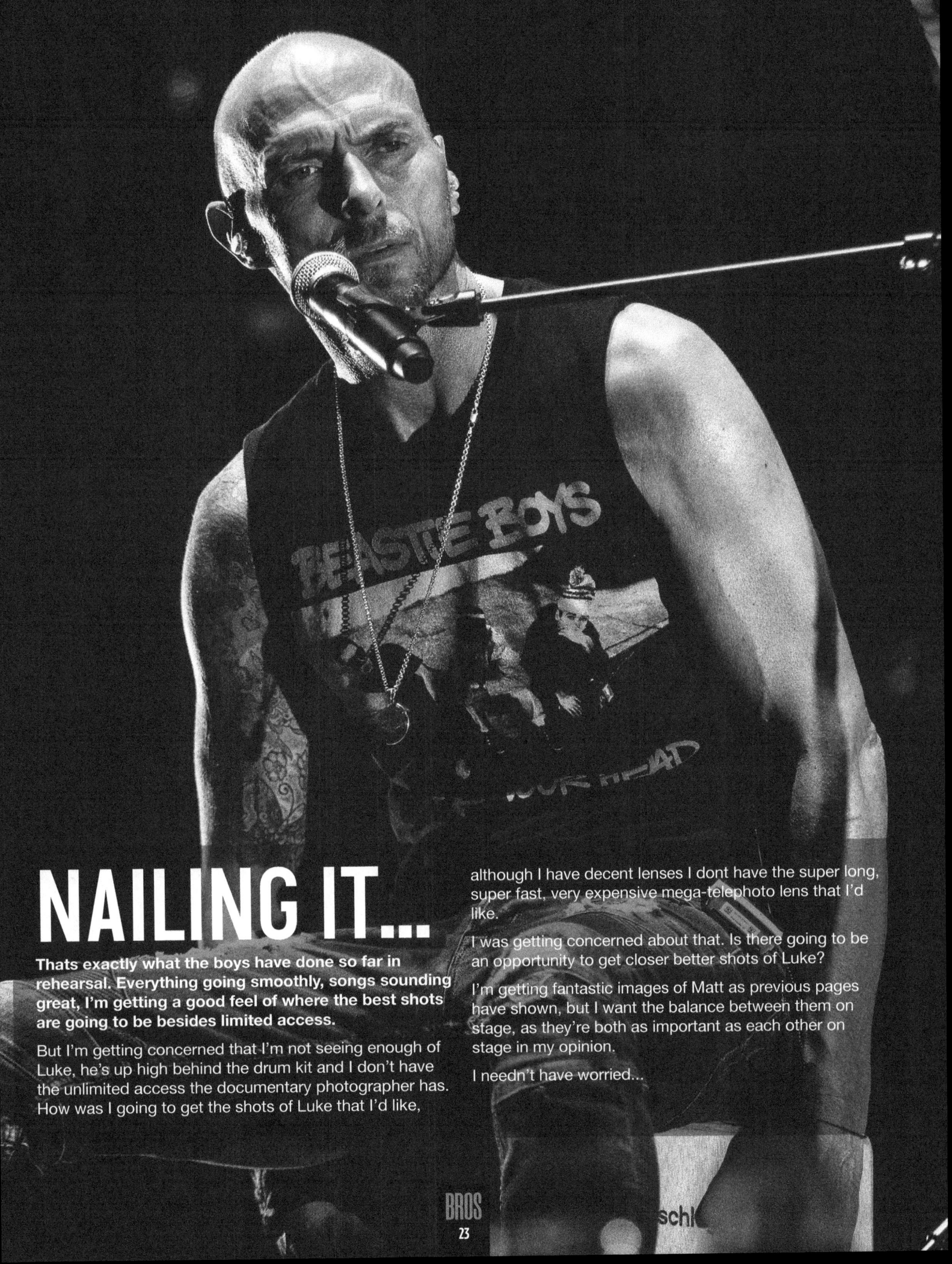

NAILING IT...

Thats exactly what the boys have done so far in rehearsal. Everything going smoothly, songs sounding great, I'm getting a good feel of where the best shots are going to be besides limited access.

But I'm getting concerned that I'm not seeing enough of Luke, he's up high behind the drum kit and I don't have the unlimited access the documentary photographer has. How was I going to get the shots of Luke that I'd like,

although I have decent lenses I dont have the super long, super fast, very expensive mega-telephoto lens that I'd like.

I was getting concerned about that. Is there going to be an opportunity to get closer better shots of Luke?

I'm getting fantastic images of Matt as previous pages have shown, but I want the balance between them on stage, as they're both as important as each other on stage in my opinion.

I needn't have worried...

MA.®

FROM BEHIND THE KIT...

Luke finally emerges, I get some really good shots of him and I'm relieved to know that come the night of the gig I'm going to get some good shots. He looks pumped, which is not surprising as he's been working really hard throughout the gig behind the kit.

He comes down to the front of the stage to do a couple of duets with Matt and I shoot some great images of them both together.

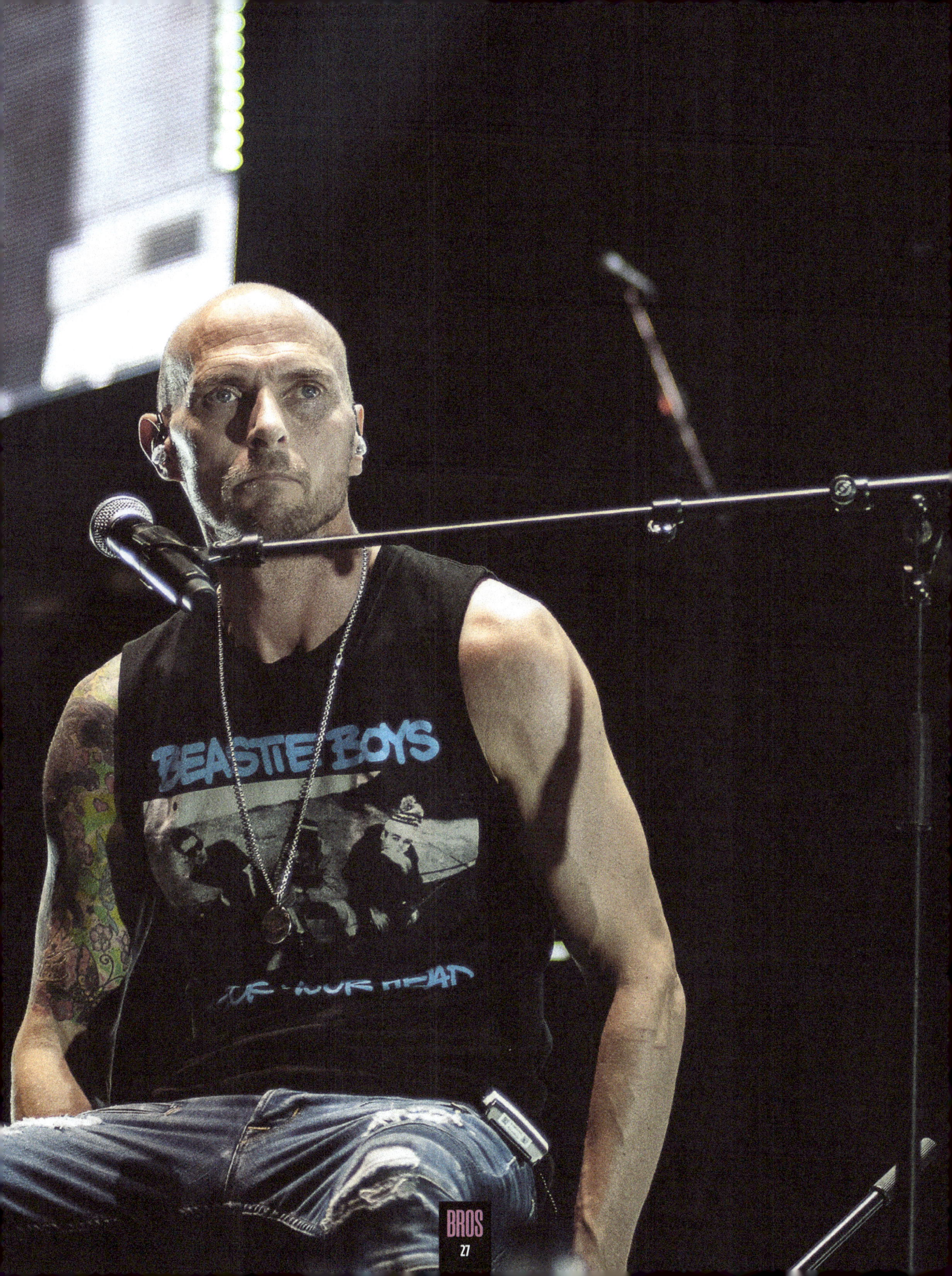

JUDGEMENT DAY ARRIVES!

The concert starts and what an opening! The boys come onto the stage through trap doors amongst a hail of smoke, the fans go wild and scream the place down, and they're still screaming at smokey silhouettes!

Then the boys lower back into the stage and emerge from different points, Luke appears near his drum kit and Matt emerges from the side, hat in hand, full of energy and purpose.

They break into "When will I be famous" straight away & the sell out crowd joins in at full blast. The atmosphere is electric & I'm getting great images. I hadn't taken into account the lightshow that was happening, as it wasn't on show in the rehearsal, its making the images look great & making the shooting process a little easier as I dont have to crop out any unsightly stuff in the background.

A brilliant start.

BLASTING THE CROWD WITH ENERGY, SOUND AND LIGHT

The boys are killing it. Luke hasn't missed a beat and Matt has the audience in the palm of his hand. The band are on point, the backing singers are sounding awesome, the bass is resonating through the bodies of the crowd.

Sounding fantastic.

THE FIRST QUARTER...

Everything has gone according to plan as the boys move into
the end of the first quarter. The crowd have been fantastic,
there are no technical issues, the crowd are begging for more.

THE SET...

It's looking and sounding amazing. The crowd are lapping it up as the boys move into the second half of the concert.

The light show looks great and is really making the images look fantastic. I know we are a few songs away from Luke coming to the front of the stage, so I begin to prepare my second camera with a wider lens to accommodate this.

In the meantime, Matt still has the audience in the palm of his hand.

A GLOWING TRIBUTE...

A glowing tribute to their much loved mother, who passed away a few years ago. Images of her were displayed on the background as they sang, along with images of their late sister.

Also images of "Brosettes" from back in the day. You could hear whoops of delight as fans recognise themselves on screen.

THE LOYAL &
THE FAITHFUL...

Of course you can't have a concert without fans, and boy are these fans loyal!

They've waited nearly thirty years for this comeback and it was worth the wait.

I couldn't photograph this concert without some images of the fans.

These fans are incredible, and as you can imagine I've seen some of them grow up before my eyes. The boys have always made time for their fans.

FREEDOM.....

The final section of the show begins & the boys are performing a fitting tribute to George Michael by performing one of his most iconic tracks "Freedom."

It's especially fitting as Luke's wife Shirley Lewis was George's friend and backing singer for over twenty-five years and sang on the recorded track. They are also joined by Don Estes, the original bass player on that track.

Quite a fitting and emotional tribute to a great artist.

The show has been fantastic, the boys certainly showed their harshest critics that they can play & they can sing.

THEY DID IT!

What a job the boys did! The concert was amazing and I found it hard to believe that it's been over twenty five years since they played together. Although I'm a friend of theirs I would've been honest and critical if I thought that it was a poor gig, after all I'm a man in his fifties who grew up on roots reggae & hip hop, but I must say they did a fantastic job.

Giving their eighties pop songs a harder, rockier sound and edge was a smart move, Luke's powerful hard beats kept the groove and edge in the songs and made them relevant whilst Matt's powerful impressive vocals kept enchantment in the melodies and his energetic stage performance kept the audience in his hands.

The stage and lighting was impressive and the whole event did exactly what it said on the tin.

I enjoyed shooting the whole event and was pleased to at last see the brothers perform together after over twenty five years of knowing them.

Will they perform together again? Hopefully.

I'd like to see them perform again, take creative chances perhaps.

Whatever they choose to do I wish them immense success and happiness.

THANKFUL...

Capturing the guys over the years has been immensely enjoyable and being here to see them perform at last has been fantastic. I hope everyone will enjoy this little insight into what it takes to create a major event like this and I've enjoyed it immensely, as I always do when creating projects like this.

There are a few people I want to thank for being able to produce this book. Although it was never my intention to produce a book of images when I shot these pictures, (I merely wanted to finish the archive I have on the guys) when the suggestion was put to me by a team member I thought it would be a mistake not to grasp the opportunity.

I'd like to thank Luke and Matt Goss for allowing me access to create these images and offer huge congratulations for a fantastic job. Immensely proud and impressed by your performances.

I'd like to thank Shirley Lewis for being a lifelong friend and thank you for instigating the production of this book.

Without your input and help this would not have been possible.

I'd like to thank Teddie at New Haven Publishing for having the interest and vision in my project.

David Wood, thank you for being a good friend & so helpful over the years, wish you'd come back to the UK man! You're sorely missed and it was so good to see you again.

Adam Philips, thank you for your undying support over the years, you too have been a good friend and I cant wait to kick your arse on the golf course!

And thank you to all the Bros fans who have enjoyed my images and for the messages of praise and support over the years.